Discovery Kids

CUTEST WILD ANIMALS OF ALL TIME

by Mari Bolte

PEBBLE
a capstone imprint

Published by Pebble, an imprint of Capstone
1710 Roe Crest Drive, North Mankato, Minnesota 56003
capstonepub.com

Library of Congress Cataloging-in-Publication Data is available on the Library of Congress website.

ISBN: 9798875256660 (hardcover)
ISBN: 9798875256615 (paperback)
ISBN: 9798875256622 (ebook PDF)

Summary: Sixteen wild animals face off in a challenge to find out which animal is the C.O.A.T.—Cutest of All Time. Each animal receives a score of one to five in three categories for an overall cute factor score.

Editorial Credits
Editor: Erika L. Shores; Designer: Dina Her; Media Researcher: Rebekah Hubstenberger; Production Specialist: Tori Abraham

Image Credits
Getty Images: DmitryND, 10 (arctic fox), Gabrielle Therin-Weise, 12 (dolphin), Gerald Corsi, 1 (left), 13, iStock/phototrip, 18, James R.D. Scott, 9, Kathleen Reeder Wildlife Photography, 19; Shutterstock: BearFotos, 14, Daniel Toh, 3 (left), 11, dwi putra stock, back cover (right), 3 (right), 8, Elen_Art, 10 (doodle scarf), Eric Isselee, front cover (middle left), 1 (right), 4, 6 (koala), 7, 15, 17 (axolotl), Fiq28, 16, hamsyafar, 14 (doodle mountain), Hideaki Edo Photography, 21 (quokka), 22, Kidside studio, front cover (doodle chef hat), KYRYCHENKO ANASTASIIA (doodle glasses), front and back cover, 4, 13, 16, lesyau_art (stars and winner ribbon), throughout, Look_Studio (doodle hearts, stars, candy, lollipop), back cover and throughout, Margaret M Stewart, 5, Mr. SUTTIPON YAKHAM, front cover (bottom middle), Nadiinko (twinkle stars), front and back cover, 1, P. SumethaAksorn, back cover (left), Pascale Gueret, front cover (bottom right), Polina Tomtosova (doodle flowers, shapes, lines, sparkle), throughout, Rebellion Works, front cover (doodle crown and wand), Supersubstd (doodle cap), 1, 6, Voin_Sveta, 21 (doodle crown), walliya silachan, 17 (doodle bow-tie), wasapohn, 12 (doodle hat), Zaie (dot background), cover and throughout

Printed and bound in China. 006460

CUTES FACE OFF

Wild animals are fierce. They are also fuzzy and sweet! But which wild animal is the Cutest Of All time (C.O.A.T.)?

We paired up 16 wild animals to face off in a who's cuter challenge. Each animal is given one to five stars in three categories. Read the book and check out each animal's total cuteness score. At the end, use the chart to discover who is the C.O.A.T.!

PALLAS'S CAT

Boing! Is that a boulder bouncing through the air? No, it's a Pallas's cat! These roly-poly wildcats rest during the day. At night, they watch and wait. When something yummy scampers by, they POUNCE!

Cutest Thing About Me:
My little grumpy face!

Fluffiness: ★★★☆☆
Aww Factor: ★★★★☆
Playfulness: ★★★☆☆

Total Cute Factor: 10

CHIPMUNK

How many snacks can you hold in your mouth at once? If you're a chipmunk, a lot! Chipmunks stick acorns, seeds, and nuts in their cheeks. Their cheeks are like built-in grocery bags. Chipmunks bring back food to their nest. They store it up for winter.

KOALA

Koalas spend their lives munching on leaves. A koala eats a big salad of **eucalyptus** leaves each day. Then, it falls asleep for the next 18 to 22 hours. Zzzzzz.

HEDGEHOG

Hello, friend! People in Europe are happy to find a hedgehog in their gardens. These spiky critters eat bugs and other pests. Some people even make nests, hoping a hedgehog will stop by.

Cutest Thing About Me:
Wet, wiggly nose!

Fluffiness: ☆☆☆☆☆
Aww Factor: ★★★★★
Playfulness: ★★★☆☆

Total Cute Factor: 8

SUGAR GLIDER

Sugar gliders leap through the air from tree to tree. They are searching for snacks! They eat bugs, eggs, and lizards. But they also sip on tree sap and flower **nectar**. Their favorite snack is a sugary, crusty tree sap called manna.

Teeny tiny toes!

Fluffiness: ★★★☆☆

Aww Factor: ★★★☆☆

Playfulness: ★★★☆☆

Total Cute Factor: 9

Cutest Thing About Me:
Silly snoot!

Fluffiness: ☆☆☆☆☆

Aww Factor: ★★★★★

Playfulness: ★★★★★

Total Cute Factor: 10

BLUE SHARK

Say cheese! Blue sharks look like they are smiling. These sharks are curious. They might swim up to divers to see if they have anything yummy to eat.

Cutest Thing About Me:
Big, bushy tail!

Fluffiness:	★★★★★
Aww Factor:	★★★☆☆
Playfulness:	★★★★☆

Total Cute Factor: 12

ARCTIC FOX

Arctic foxes live where it's very cold. To keep warm, they snuggle deep in the snow. Their fluffy tails wrap around their bodies like a blanket. They tuck their noses in when they get too chilly.

ADÉLIE PENGUIN

Adélie penguins are little but fierce. Sometimes they chase away predators. They have even booped human researchers with their fins!

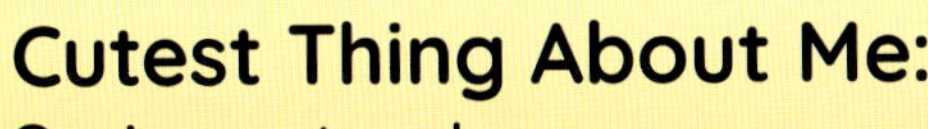

Cutest Thing About Me:
Serious stare!

Fluffiness: 1 of 5 stars
Aww Factor: 2 of 5 stars
Playfulness: 4 of 5 stars

Total Cute Factor: 7

PINK RIVER DOLPHIN

Most dolphins live in the ocean. But pink river dolphins live in the Amazon River! They are born gray but turn pink over time. No one is quite sure why. But scientists do know that males are pinker than females.

Cutest Thing About Me:
Pink skin!

Fluffiness: ☆☆☆☆☆
Aww Factor: ★★★☆☆
Playfulness: ★★★☆☆

Total Cute Factor: 6

Cutest Thing About Me:
Wispy whiskers!

Fluffiness: ★★☆☆☆
Aww Factor: ★★★★★
Playfulness: ★★★★☆

Total Cute Factor: 11

SEA OTTER

Sea otters spend most of their lives floating in the ocean. They sleep in groups while holding paws. Large groups of sleeping otters are called rafts. Rafts keep otters warm. They also make sure no otter drifts away.

MOUNTAIN GOAT

Mountain goats climb up high in rocky mountains. A wooly, white coat keeps them warm. Long shaggy fur grows on their legs. They look like they are wearing short pants.

Cutest Thing About Me:
White beard!

Fluffiness: ★★★☆☆

Aww Factor: ★★★☆☆

Playfulness: ★★★☆☆

Total Cute Factor: 9

Cutest Thing About Me:
Babies are called pufflings!

Fluffiness: ★☆☆☆☆

Aww Factor: ★★★★☆

Playfulness: ★★★☆☆

Total Cute Factor: 8

PUFFIN

What animal looks like a duck and a penguin? A puffin! These seabirds have bodies shaped like footballs. What else makes these birds cute? Orange **beaks** and feet!

Cutest Thing About Me:
Little nose and eyes!

Fluffiness: ★★★★☆
Aww Factor: ★★★★★
Playfulness: ★★★☆☆

Total Cute Factor: 12

RED PANDA

Red pandas are about the same size as a pet cat. When they are scared or surprised, they stand up straight. They make themselves look as tall as possible. Then, they put their front paws in the air. So big and scary and CUTE!

AXOLOTL

Most **salamanders** live in water and on land. But adorable axolotls live in the water full time. They breathe with feathery **gills** on the side of their heads. They can also breathe through their skin.

Cutest Thing About Me:
Supersweet smile!

Fluffiness: ☆☆☆☆☆

Aww Factor: ★★★★☆

Playfulness: ★★★★☆

Total Cute Factor: 8

QUOKKA

Is it a cat? Is it a rat? No, it's a quokka! Quokkas have round ears and a hairless tail. When they run, they bound and hop kind of like a bunny. But quokkas are **marsupials**. That means they also have a pouch.

Cutest Thing About Me:
Amazingly adorable grin!

Fluffiness: ★★★☆☆

Aww Factor: ★★★★★

Playfulness: ★★★★★

Total Cute Factor: 13

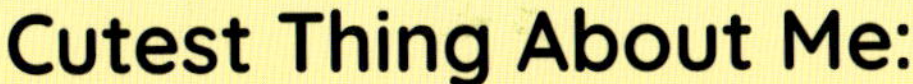

Cutest Thing About Me:
Fuzzy wuzzy feet!

Fluffiness: ★★★★★
Aww Factor: ★★★★★
Playfulness: ★★☆☆☆

Total Cute Factor: 12

SNOW LEOPARD

Snow leopards live in the mountains of Asia. They leap from rock to rock with ease. Their long tails help them stay balanced. Snow leopards are about the length of a couch. But half their length is just their tails!

CUTE FACTOR FACE OFF

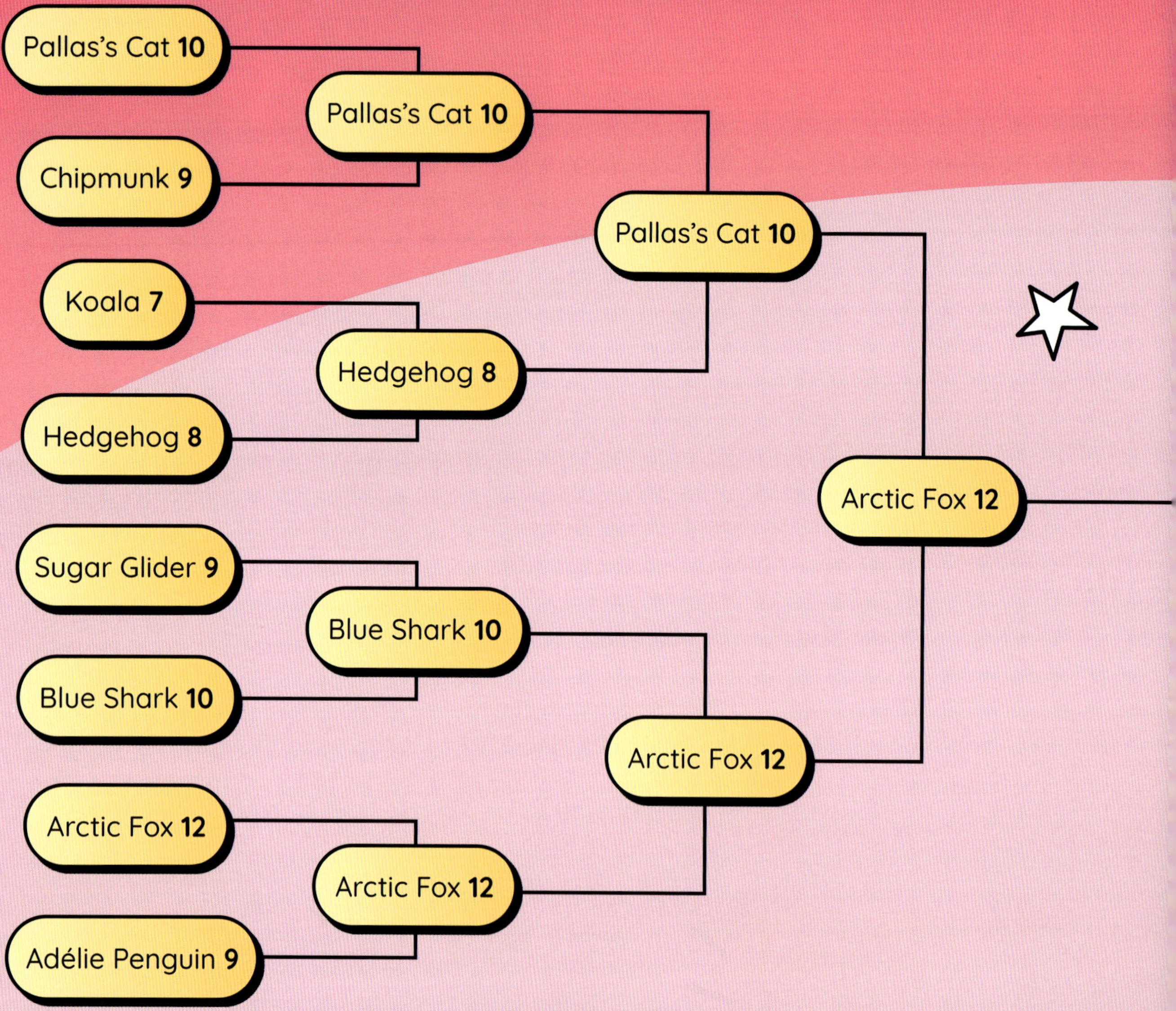

Pallas's Cat **10**

Chipmunk **9**

Pallas's Cat **10**

Koala **7**

Hedgehog **8**

Hedgehog **8**

Pallas's Cat **10**

Sugar Glider **9**

Blue Shark **10**

Blue Shark **10**

Arctic Fox **12**

Adélie Penguin **9**

Arctic Fox **12**

Arctic Fox **12**

Arctic Fox **12**

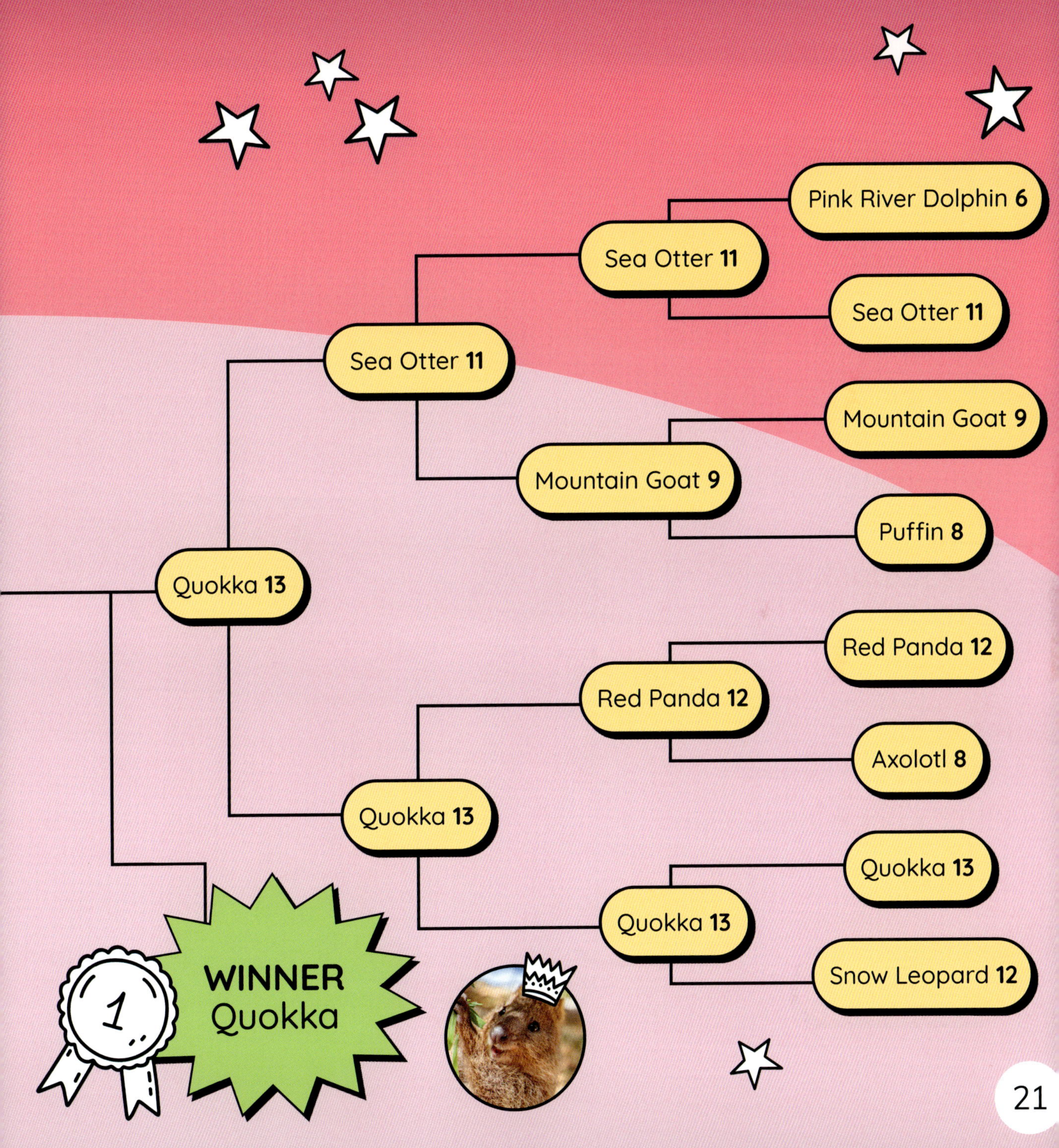
Pink River Dolphin 6
Sea Otter 11
Sea Otter 11
Sea Otter 11
Mountain Goat 9
Mountain Goat 9
Puffin 8
Quokka 13
Red Panda 12
Red Panda 12
Axolotl 8
Quokka 13
Quokka 13
Quokka 13
Snow Leopard 12
1
WINNER
Quokka

THE C.O.A.T.

This smiling face is wildly adorable and supersweet. It's official: Quokkas are the Cutest Of All Time!

Do you agree? Go back and give each animal your own score. Grab a piece of paper and make a new chart. Maybe a different animal will be your winner.

GLOSSARY

beak (BEEK)—the hard front part of the mouth of birds

eucalyptus (yoo-kuh-LIP-tuhs)—evergreen trees in the myrtle family; also known as gum trees

gill (GIL)—a body part on the side of a fish; fish use their gills to breathe

marsupial (mar-SOO-pee-uhl)—a group of mammals in which the females feed and carry their young in pouches

nectar (NEK-tuhr)—a sweet liquid found in many flowers

salamander (SAL-uh-man-duhr)—a lizard-like amphibian with a long body, a long tail, and short limbs

INDEX

ABOUT THE AUTHOR

Mari Bolte is the author and editor of hundreds of children's books. Every book is her favorite book as long as the readers learned something and enjoyed themselves!